Contents

Chapter 1: Understanding M.E

Chapter 2: Rest & Pacing

Chapter 3: Diet & Nutrition

Chapter 4: Sleep

Chapter 5: Vitamins & Supplements

Chapter 6: Healthcare & Medication

Chapter 7: Friends, Family & relationships

Chapter 8: Self Care

Chapter 9: Welfare Support

Chapter 10: Emotional Aspects

Chapter 11: Alternative Therapies

Chapter 12: Symptomatic Relief

Chapter 13: Hobbies

Chapter 14: Summary

© 2013 Hayley Green. All rights reserved.

ISBN 978-1-291-57545-3

Chapter 1: Understanding M.E

What Is M.E?

Myalgic Encephalomyelitis is a long term disabling condition which can cause long term illness. It fluctuates in nature and no every one patient has the same set of symptoms. Myalgic means muscle pain and inflammation, and Encephalomyelitis means inflammation of the brain and spinal cord. It is often referred to as CFS (Chronic Fatigue Syndrome) or PVFS (Post Viral Fatigue Syndrome). Many sufferers prefer to use the term Myalgic Encephalomyelitis rather than Chronic Fatigue Syndrome, as the fatigue is much more than normal 'tiredness', and whereas fatigue may be a prominent symptom, the condition has a multitude of other debilitating symptoms along with it.

What Causes M.E?

Although there are several scientific theories, the cause of the illness remains unknown. Some experts believe it is triggered by a viral infection, such as tonsillitis. Others believe it is an auto-immune condition, or metabolic disorder. There appears to be a trigger in most cases, and there are factors believed to contribute to some people developing M.E – including genetic susceptibility, emotional stress and traumatic life events such as bereavement. Factors believed to make M.E worse are recurring viral and bacterial infections, stress and poor diet.

What Are The Symptoms?

Symptoms often fluctuate in intensity and can vary day to day, or even hour to hour. Common symptoms include:

- Fatigue - It is very different to every day tiredness, such as from a long day at work, which for most people would be relieved from an early night. It is not relieved by sleep or rest.

- Headaches – Persistent headaches, a pressure feeling on the head which some describe as a feeling as if your head has been put in a vice. These appear to be tension headaches in most cases and are accompanied by tense neck muscles.

- Muscle Pain (Myalgia) – This is often described as a deep burning pain, and can be accompanied by muscle spasms, soreness and weakness.

- Post-exertional malaise – This is an important factor which identifies M.E from many other illnesses. A sufferer will feel an increase in symptoms after an increase in activity, and this generally manifests 24-48 hours after the activity. So even on a 'better' day, when a sufferer feels they can do more, they can overdo it and be paying for it in terms of an increase in symptoms for days or even weeks afterwards. This is what M.E suffers call a 'crash'.

- Symptoms which suggest immune system abnormality - These include sore throats, sweating, inability for the body to regulate temperature and flu like symptoms.

- Depression, mood swings and anxiety - These are common in the illness, due to the effects of symptoms on mental health and the significant lifestyle changes it can cause. Some people feel a loss for their old life, and it is natural to go through a grieving process after being diagnosed. Many can feel irritable and upset easily.

- Cognitive Issues – Suffers report problems with memory loss, ability to concentrate, forgetfulness and word finding abilities. Feeling spaced out and disorientated, and having problems with co –ordination are also common.

- Palpitations – Where the sufferer feels the heart pounding in the chest

- Digestive Issues such as Irritable Bowel Syndrome, are conditions which often go 'hand in hand' with M.E. These can cause bloating, diarrhoea and constipation.

Other symptoms include, but are not limited to, the below. Some are more common than others.

- Fainting and seizures
- Blurred vision
- Very low blood pressure especially when standing
- Stroke or Coma-like episodes
- Nausea and vomiting
- Feeling 'poisoned'
- Food allergies and chemical sensitivities
- Alcohol intolerance
- Pallor of face
- Enlarged lymph nodes
- Vertigo

How Is It Diagnosed?

There is no test for M.E. The illness is diagnosed by a GP using a patient's medical history, assessing the symptoms against the typical pattern of symptoms of M.E, and by ruling out other illnesses which may cause similar symptoms. A sufferer must have had the symptoms for at least 6 months before a diagnosis can be considered.

How Common Is It?

There are around 250,000 people in the UK who have M.E, including men, women and children. It is more common in women than men, and although the most common age for people to develop the illness is between the ages of 20 and 40 years of age, it can affect anyone of any age.

Most cases are mild to moderate, but a small percentage who suffer severely are completely bedbound, and a significant amount are housebound.

There is currently no cure for M.E, although research is ongoing. This book will help you learn how to cope with the illness in all aspects of your life, from the eyes of a fellow sufferer.

What Is A Crash?

A 'crash' is a term often used by sufferers to describe the way their bodies react when they have done too much, either physically or mentally. For someone with the condition, a face to face conversation can be just as exhausting as a short walk. Mental function requires energy just as much as physical exertion. M.E sufferers crash when they push past their limits, limits which are different for everyone depending on whether they are mild, moderately or severely affected. A crash will bring on an increase in symptoms such as fatigue and pain, and it can last a few hours, or it can last for days and even months depending on how far the sufferer has pushed past their boundaries.

What Is Sensory Overload?

Sensory overload is a very significant part of many sufferers' symptoms. Any of the senses can be a source of sensory overload, including noises, lights and smells and can lead to an increase in symptoms and irritability. Symptoms of the illness relating to sensory overload are noise and light sensitivity. Sounds are far more audible to that of a non-sufferer and can often be overwhelming. Someone talking at a normal level can sound like shouting and when a sufferer is experiencing a crash this is magnified. The sound of a piece of paper being scrunched up can be too much to bear. Some sufferers who are severely affected and bedbound are very sensitive to sound and light, and need to stay in a darkened room, with no light or noise.

Chapter 2: Rest & Pacing

1. **Adequate rest** – Perhaps before you became unwell, rest meant watching a film, or reading a book. When you have M.E, even these activities take up energy you don't have, due to sensory overload. Although everyone has different levels of fatigue and as such different rest requirements, you need to find an activity that restores energy for you. The best way to do this is through meditation or simply laying down in a dark room with no noise or light.
2. **Balancing rest & activity** – One of the best pieces of advice I received about pacing was to look at your energy like a battery. A healthy person would expect to wake up and have a fully charged battery. By the end of the day they would still have plenty of 'battery power' left. With M.E, it doesn't work like this. Everything you do takes a huge chunk of that battery power, and it empties at a much quicker rate than it would if you were healthy. A rule of the thumb is that for every thirty minutes of activity, get thirty minutes of rest afterwards. Of course you may need more than thirty minutes, as everyone is different.
3. **Finding A Baseline** – Everyone with the condition has a different baseline. This is the point at which you can use energy to carry out an activity, without an increase in symptoms. Quite simply, an increase in symptoms means that you have pushed past your limits. On some days this may mean just getting out of bed, on others it could be a 5 minute call to a friend half way through the day. If you are experiencing an increase in symptoms regularly due to overdoing it, you will not get better. A useful technique is to set your baseline to around 50% of what you feel you can do on an average day.
4. **Increasing Activity** – Once you have found your baseline, and stick to it, meaning that you get to a point where you can get through the day without 'crashing' – the idea is that then you gradually increase activity. It is important to get a balance between increasing the activity level without bringing on an increase in symptoms. At first you may feel a slight increase, as your body adjusts, but if you feel yourself becoming very unwell then this is a clear indicator that it is too much, so that is a time to go back to basics and find your baseline. When you decide to increase an activity, do these at no more than 10%. For example this may mean than instead of doing 10 minutes of activity, do 11 minutes.
5. **Adjusting to lifestyle factors** – Life can be unpredictable, and something such as stress, or a big upheaval such as a house move, can completely throw you out of sync with your pacing. Some events are unavoidable, and it is times like this you need to do as

little else as possible in order to deal with the unexpected. Apply pacing to everything you do, so break up activities as much as possible, and ensure that you incorporate valuable rest time into it. If you need help, ask for it. If you do feel you have done too much, then rest as much as possible until you are feeling better. A days rest is far more worthwhile than carrying on for longer and potentially being in bed for days.

6. **Managing setbacks** – Setbacks can happen in all walks of life. M.E is a fluctuating illness and relapses are common. If you do relapse then do not blame yourself. Instead look at every aspect of your life including, rest, activity, stress and environmental factors. Have you been getting good quality sleep? Have you really been sticking to your baseline? Be honest with yourself and try and identify what is having a negative effect on your state of health. Unless you know what is contributing to relapses, you will not be able to correct it further on.

7. **Meditation** – One of the best forms of relaxation is Meditation. This enables your body and your mind to relax completely and in the case of M.E this is essential when it comes to rest. Books, Cd's and even Mobile phone applications offer many different programs – you may need to try a few different ones to find one that works best for you, but when you do the results can be very rewarding. Often the symptoms of a crash can be lessened by putting your mind and body into a state of tranquility and this enables you to get a bit of energy back into that 'battery'.

8. **Priorities** – Many people with the illness are driven, enthusiastic people with high achievements and goals. When you are diagnosed with such an illness it can be very difficult to put tasks on the back burner. However in order to recover you must not push past your limits. This is a sure fire way of a relapse if you try and ignore the symptoms and 'push through'. It may be tempting to do 'just one more thing' at the end of the day, but that one more thing can be the difference between going to bed not feeling too bad or going to bed crashing, and possibly for days. A good question to ask yourself when you feel tempted to continue something when you know you should be resting, is – Does my life depend on it? In 99.9% of cases the answer is no! You may have been able to carry out a multitude of tasks in one day previously, but in order to set the standards for recovery, accepting that you cannot do as much as you used to is

paramount. This of course doesn't mean to say that you should neglect everything, but recognizing when your body has had enough is vital.

9. **How to relax** – Ensure you have a quiet environment with no distractions. It is best to lay down to ensure your whole body is in a comfortable position, and make sure you are warm enough as the temperature of your body can lower during relaxation. Breathing is an important part of relaxation, breathe deeply and slowly and you will soon feel this helps your physical self to relax too. Relaxation music can be helpful but sometimes you may need silence. Notice how your muscles feel when you are mentally relaxed and once you recognize this it will be easier to get into the relaxed state.

10. **Relaxation Techniques** - There are many relaxation techniques available and you just need to find which works best for you. Effective techniques include: Breathing, visualization, meditation, aromatherapy, massage and hypnosis.

Chapter 3: Diet & Nutrition

11. **Basic Nutrition** - A healthy diet is essential for managing the condition. Eating healthily can contribute to energy levels and boost the immune system. A balanced diet is important for anyone, and many experts recommend eating Dairy, grains, fruit, vegetables and protein. Protein is especially important in this case, as this is what your body needs for both growth and maintenance.
12. **Food allergies** - Avoiding the wrong foods is as important as eating the right foods. Many people who suffer from M.E also have food allergies, and Irritable Bowel Syndrome is common. A food diary can be useful to identify the triggers to an increase in symptoms and then eliminating the culprits.
13. **Things to avoid** - Although these are generally what we should avoid in our diets whether we are healthy or not, they are especially important if you have this condition. Common symptom triggers are high calorie or greasy foods, alcohol and caffeine as well as foods high in sugar. It is recommended to eat as much fresh produce as possible and minimize processed foods.
14. **Super foods** - You may have heard of the term 'super food'. This is a modern saying for a food which is extremely nutritious and has great health benefits. An example of this is Acai Berry which is high in anti-oxidants and fibre. Berries in particular are high in anti-oxidants and there have been reports of raised energy levels with regular intake.
15. **Avoiding the 'after dinner' crash** – If you ask anyone what they feel like after a huge meal, the response will usually be 'stuffed and tired!!'. This is no different if you have M.E, in fact it is worse. Overeating puts a huge strain on the digestive system and will often bring on a huge increase in fatigue. It has been recommended to eat little and often to balance energy levels and avoid feeling awful after dinner, which can often trigger the 'evening crash' that most sufferers will be familiar with.
16. **Losing weight** - M.E can make it incredibly difficult to lose weight. Factors which may contribute to this include lack of good quality sleep, stress and a decrease in physical activity due to the nature of the illness. However extreme diets are not the answer. Although it may be tempting to go on a very low calorie diet, there is no use being

slender if you can't go out and show your figure off! The bottom line is that a crash diet is likely to impact on your overall health and this is something which must come first.

Chapter 4: Sleep

17. **Good quality sleep** – Sleep is essential for good health. Many sufferers have a poor quality of sleep. This can include difficulty getting to sleep or staying asleep. Sleep is unrefreshing and sufferers often wake up groggy the next morning. There are medications your GP can prescribe which can help you get to sleep, or to improve quality of sleep. These are detailed further on in the chapter on medications. Trying to get as good quality sleep as possible is very important.
18. **Mind chatter** – Often it is difficult to get to sleep due to an overactive mind. This is where meditation helps. Clearing your mind and relaxing your whole body can help you prepare for sleep, and it also helps to relieve stress and tension.
19. **Noise** – Where noise sensitivity is an issue, it can be very frustrating when sleep is concerned. Good quality sleep is extremely important if you have the condition, for just a few days of sleep deprivation is a sure fire way to send you well on the way to a relapse. Ear plugs are used by many sufferers to block out noise, and there are many types available including those designed for smaller ears.
20. **A regular bedtime** – Going to bed at a regular time every evening is recommended. This helps the body get used to the sleep pattern and gives you a routine. Some evenings, or even days, you may of course need to go much earlier. Some days you may not even be able to leave the bed, but where you can, sticking to some sort of routine can certainly be helpful not only physically but mentally too.
21. **Sleeping tablets** – Your GP may recommend prescription sleeping tablet to help you to fall or stay asleep. However these may have side effects. If this is a concern there are many herbal alternatives available over the counter.
22. **Sleep environment** – In order to help achieve a good quality sleeping pattern, a comfortable environment is essential. Ensure you have a comfortable mattress, which is the correct type for you. Some sufferers find memory foam or orthopedic mattresses help, and a good quality mattress can be a great investment. Also ensuring the room is at a comfortable temperature for you is important. If the room is too warm then this will just exacerbate hot sweats during the night.

23. **Pain during sleep** – Often pain is worse during the evening hours. If muscle pain is an issue then deep heat before bed can often help, as can a self-massage machine.

Chapter 5 – Vitamins & Supplements

24. **Multivitamins** – Often we don't get all of the essential vitamins and minerals that our bodies need through diet. A daily multivitamin is a good starting point if you have M.E, many sufferers have reported improvements through using Multivitamins.
25. **Co-Enzyme Q-10** – This is an antioxidant found naturally within the body. It is required for functioning of cells and energy production. Some sufferers have been found to be deficient, so this is a good supplement to take.
26. **Vitamin C** – An essential nutrient with a variety of uses within the body, this is something that our bodies cannot store and therefore should be taken daily, especially in the case of chronic illness. Vitamin C is beneficial to the immune system and is a powerful antioxidant. 2000mg daily is recommended for those suffering from M.E.
27. **D-Ribose** – A natural sugar provided by the body, D-Ribose enhances energy production within the cells and can help with muscle recovery. This can be purchased in both powder and tablet form, depending on what suits you best. This is especially important with M.E because the energy production within the body is not performing to a normal standard. Studies have shown that D-Ribose can increase energy levels.
28. **L-Carnitine** – This is an amino acid which is naturally occurring within almost all cells of the body and has been lauded to help fight fatigue. It has been proven to benefit some M.E patients.
29. **Magnesium** – A very important mineral for the body, Magnesium has many health benefits and plays a large role in the body's detoxification process. It can also help to regulate blood sugar levels and high blood sugar, keep bones strong and ease stress and tension. The mineral comes in many different forms including salts (More often referred to as 'Epsom salts') which can be added to bath water; the Magnesium is then absorbed through the skin. There are also oil forms, and as Magnesium helps to relax muscles the oil can be applied directly to the muscle and rubbed in to help pain and muscle soreness.
30. **Omega-3** - Found in oily fish, this is called an 'essential' supplement as it is not found naturally within the body. It can contribute to heart, vision and brain function. Where cognitive issues can be a significant symptom of M.E, this is a recommended supplement to take.

Chapter 6: Healthcare & Medication

31. **Finding a supportive GP** – Unfortunately a lot of sufferers have found their GP does not have the knowledge or understanding of the illness to be able to provide full support. If you find your GP is unsupportive then it is a good idea to look for another one. With such a complex illness you need as much support as possible and unfortunately more often than not GP's are quite uneducated when it comes to M.E. It would be helpful to contact local surgeries and ask whether they have any practitioners who have a special interest in the condition.
32. **Consultant referrals** – Unfortunately the services for individuals with the condition in the UK vary depending on the area. Some counties have a specialist clinic to which sufferers can be referred to, but some do not have these facilities. If you feel you need further support than what your GP can provide then do not feel afraid to ask to be referred to a specialist in the area if this is available.
33. **Support groups** – Across the UK there are many support groups for M.E sufferers. If you are able to get out then this is a great opportunity to meet others who understand exactly what you are dealing with. Some of these provide regular recreational meetings and events for sufferers and their families/carers. An internet search can provide further details of a group in a location near to you.
34. **Pain medication** – Several over the counter pain remedies can be helpful when it comes to managing pain with M.E. These include paracetamol, ibuprofen and co-codamol. For muscle pain Diclofenac can be especially helpful as it is an anti-inflammatory drug. It is important to find a drug which helps you, but if you feel over the counter medications are not helping your pain then your GP should be able to advise you on other options.
35. **Amitriptyline** – This is a tricyclic anti-depressant often used as a sedative analgesic in lower doses for many M.E sufferers to help manage pain. As it can make you sleepy it is usually taken at night. Ask your GP about this medication if pain is a big issue and you find other pain medications are not effective.
36. **Private GPs** – If you are struggling to find a supportive or understanding GP then finding a private GP may be an option if you have the means. There are GPs who specialise in the condition who can be contacted online. Further information can be found in the 'useful contacts' section of this book

Chapter 7: Friends, Family & Relationships

37. **How to explain the fatigue** – Being an 'invisible' illness, a significant proportion of sufferers find that it is difficult to explain to relatives and friends. Unfortunately because sometimes we can 'look' okay, people can too often assume that we also 'feel' okay, but this is not the case. Being diagnosed with a debilitating illness we need the support from our family and friends the most. It is hard to describe what having the condition feels like, but a good way to describe it is to ask the person to remember a time they had the flu. The exhaustion that you feel when you have the flu is much more than just 'normal' tiredness, and getting out of bed is a struggle. Your whole body aches, and the fatigue is bone shattering. Ask them to imagine they had run a marathon, and had not slept for a week, along with a hangover – this is what M.E feels like day in day out. Explain that whilst the fatigue from the flu would soon disappear, with this condition it never goes away and it is permanent from the moment you wake to the moment you go to sleep.
38. **Coping with ignorant comments** – Although friends and family can be well meaning, sometimes they can say things which someone with the illness will find highly offensive. They may think they are being supportive when they tell you 'I get tired too', but the fatigue experienced by someone with this illness is far more than the tiredness that a healthy person would feel after a long day's work. Explain to them that it is not the kind of tiredness that can be relieved by an early night or a holiday. It is an unnatural severe exhaustion that controls every aspect of your life and is not relieved by any amount of sleep or rest.
39. **Exercise and M.E** – For a lot of illnesses, exercise can be very beneficial. However for M.E sufferers it can be dangerous. Sometimes people may suggest getting some exercise – but you need to make them understand that whilst exercise is beneficial for a lot of illnesses, in this case it is not. Explain that one of the main symptoms of the illness is Post-exertional malaise. The body is exercise intolerant, and depending on how severe the illness is, it can do serious harm to a sufferer's health. It may take time for people to understand the nature of the illness, but if they are not mature enough to be able to understand the difference in abilities between a healthy person and someone with M.E, then this is not your problem. Unfortunately not everyone will understand, and it can be

both upsetting and stressful – after all, if someone cares about you then you would expect them to research in order that they do understand. But if this is not the case do not let it get you down. You are the one who has to live with the illness, the last thing you need on top of that is ignorance and lack of understanding. A helpful way to explain the nature of M.E is that when we wake up in the morning, we have a 'battery'. Healthy people will have a full battery, let's say 100%, and this will perhaps only be half empty by the end of a long day, leaving plenty left at the end of the evening. People with M.E wake up with their battery already almost on 'empty'. Everything they do thereafter takes away a huge chunk of that little energy they have, delving into 'emergency' energy reserves, and that battery runs down at a much faster rate than a healthy person. Every activity rapidly uses that energy, and makes the sufferer feel worse, bringing on an increase in symptoms such as malaise, fatigue and pain.

40. **Socialising** – Before you became ill you may have had an active social life, being able to go out and meet friends or go to parties. Now even getting through the day is exhausting. A lot of sufferers find they lose friends due to not being able to go out and do the things they used to be able to do before they were sick. If they are a friend worth having then they will make the effort to learn about your illness and support you the best they can. If they are not supportive and lose interest in you then this just shows the kind of person they are, and it is best to keep your distance.

41. **Asking for help** – It can be hard to ask for help. Especially if previously you were an independent person! But being unwell means that you cannot do as much as you used to be able to, and it is hard to admit that, however do not feel guilty if you need to ask for help. It may be a small task that needs doing, and as we know those small tasks can be exhausting. So don't be afraid to accept that sometimes you may need some help from family or friends, as you would more than likely do exactly the same if it were the other way round.

42. **How the illness can affect others** – Just as upsetting as it can be for us being diagnosed, it can be equally as upsetting for the people close to you. The once lively, independent and fun loving person they knew is now severely restricted and big changes have had to be made. Recognise that whilst not everyone will admit it, they need support too in dealing with your diagnosis. Communication is essential in every relationship whether it be friends, family or partners – and it is important to ensure the people close to you are able to cope, especially if they play a big role in caring for you. Making sure

they have someone to turn to is important and also be ready to answer any questions about the condition, to help them understand the nature of the illness.

Chapter 8: Self Care

43. **Washing** – Sometimes we are so exhausted we neglect our self care. Whereas a bath is great for aching muscles, it can take too much energy to have one. If you usually shower but find standing up for too long is too much then a bath would be more appropriate. Some days you will find even a bath is too tiring. There are lots of products that will help you to keep and feel clean – baby wipes and deodorant serve well in place of a bath until you feel better
44. **Washing your hair** – For men or ladies with shorter hair this may not be so much of an issue to go a few days without washing it. Sometimes I myself go for two weeks without washing my hair, as by the time the evening comes I am feeling far too unwell to even consider it. There are various dry shampoo products out there which will help keep your hair cleaner and more manageable until you can get to wash it.
45. **Brushing your teeth** – M.E sufferers know all too well how weak their arms can get by holding things. And sometimes even the movement of brushing your teeth can be all too much. An electric toothbrush is fantastic for this, it reduces the arm movements you usually need to make with a standard toothbrush. If you feel standing up for two minutes is too much then sit down whilst brushing your teeth, make things easier for yourself wherever possible.
46. **Toilet issues** – We all know how exhausting a big crash can be. Your body is like a dead weight, and even getting out of bed to go to the toilet can be a task. This is even more so if your bathroom is considerable distance from your bedroom. Investing in a portable toilet aid can make these times much easier, and save depleting your energy further whilst you are recovering. This can also be handy if your only toilet is upstairs and depending on how much you go to the toilet, will save you energy which you would be wasting by going up and down stairs.
47. **Dealing with Periods** – If you are a lady you will know that there is a time of the month when all goes awry and as well as feeling generally angry and tearful, you may also have painful cramps to deal with too on top of your M.E symptoms. Keep a hot water bottle to hand to help with cramps, and realize that you may well feel a bit more under the weather around this time. Ensure you have painkillers handy which are effective in treating period pain.
48. **Dressing** – For an M.E sufferer it is quite normal to stay in your bedclothes and there isn't anything wrong with this. I find that on a bad day I make a point of staying in my

bed clothes, and on a better day I get dressed, this sets the mindset and helps me to take it easy when I need to, but motivates me to do a little more when I am feeling a bit better.

49. **Hair removal** – Shaving your legs can be a real chore when you have a chronic illness. If you cannot get out a lot and it doesn't worry you then leave it 'au naturel'! But if you like to be hair free then hair removal cream can be very helpful. As you will know, sufferers injure themselves very easily - I have pulled a muscle before just leaning over in the bath to shave my legs!

50. **Keeping warm** – As we all know, temperature can be an issue. Where our bodies cannot regulate temperature properly we can find we get extremely hot, or cold, in normal environments. If you get cold easily then invest in a pair of thermal socks – as old fashioned as they sound, they are very comfortable and keeping your feet warm helps your entire body stay warm. For those of you who are sweating and usually very warm, a mini hand held or desk fan can help a lot especially in the hot weather, which often causes symptoms to flare up.

51. **Eating** – Some days we can be too fatigued to even think about eating. If you are too exhausted to make breakfast, a food replacement shake can supplement this. Have some handy for the days where you are hungry, but too ill to prepare food. If you have someone in your household who helps with this, it's not such an issue – but not every sufferer has that option, so stocking up on microwave meals can be helpful and much less demanding than a meal cooked from scratch.

Chapter 9: Welfare support

52. **Should you claim** - If you are working whilst suffering from the condition, you may be struggling greatly. The question you need to ask yourself is – Is work making my condition deteriorate? If the answer is yes then you need to think about claiming the support you deserve. If your health is deteriorating through working full time then negotiating part time hours with your employer can be useful. If part time is too much for you then it may be time to stop work and put your health first.
53. **How to claim** - To claim a sickness related benefit, you will need a medical certificate from your GP. Make an appointment and explain the symptoms which you feel are affecting your ability to work. Making a diary can be helpful to show how the condition affects your daily activities.
54. **What can you claim** - Employment and support Allowance (ESA) replaced Incapacity Benefit, the out of work sickness benefit. If you are ill or disabled, it can provide financial support, and if you are able to do some kind of work, it also offers personalised help. Once your GP has signed you off, you have an assessment phase where initially you will need to complete a medical questionnaire, and after that you may be invited to a medical assessment.
55. **Personal Independence Payment** – This is a non means tested benefit formerly called Disability Living Allowance. It is a benefit designed to help cover the associated costs of living with chronic illness or disability. For example these may be related to transport and/or self-care. This involves an assessment to work out whether you are entitled to help, and if so how much you are entitled to based on the help you need.
56. **Assistance with welfare support** – You may have someone close to you who can assist in applying for sickness related benefits, but sometimes this is not the case. Professional advice is always recommended in any case as the forms can be confusing and overwhelming, especially if you suffer from cognitive difficulties. There are M.E charities and support groups which can assist with benefits advice, and also a good place to contact is the C.A.B. (Citizens Advice Bureau). Further information on contacts who can assist you with your application are listed at the end of this book under 'Useful contacts'.

Chapter 10: Emotional Aspects

57. **Depression** – This is a common symptom of M.E and can make symptoms worse, as psychological stress exhausts the adrenal glands. Many sufferers are put on anti-depressants to help them cope with the emotional aspects of having the illness. If you feel you have depression then a visit to your GP will no doubt pay off. For some this may have been an illness that preceded the M.E, for others it may develop afterwards.
58. **Anxiety** – Another common symptom of the illness, this can be overwhelming and frightening for the sufferer. Again if you feel you have anxiety which is affecting you significantly, then it's time to visit your GP.
59. **Irritability** – This can be caused both by stress and physical factors. When you are feeling very poorly for a good percentage of the time it is natural to become easily irritated, especially by loud noises or busy atmospheres'. Try and avoid the situations where you know you will find it an issue. Stress reducing techniques can also assist with this.
60. **Mood swings** – Since becoming ill you may have noticed that you have mood swings, and mood does appear to be altered as part of the biological process when M.E is developed. This can be similar to how you feel when recovering from a viral infection. It is quite normal for a sufferer to experience these from time to time.
61. **Stress** – A huge factor in our lives, stress is often unavoidable. But it is how we deal with it that counts. It is well documented that stress makes the physical symptoms of M.E worse, and can contribute to relapses. Experts know that the levels of stress hormones (Cortisol, for example) are lower than that of people without the illness, and it is believed that this is what makes it harder for sufferers to deal with stress. You may have heard of 'fight-or-flight'. This is the body's natural response to external stressors, where stress hormones such as adrenaline are released into the body, and where your body prepares for survival. If this continues over a long period, this suppresses the immune system and therefore makes it harder for the body to heal. This is thought to be why ongoing stress can be a preceding factor to the illness.
62. **Adrenaline** – A hormone released by the body in situations with the potential for danger, it is referred to as the 'flight or fight hormone'. People with M.E can often operate above their levels of physical and mental ability for certain periods of time due to the adrenaline that is being released by the adrenal gland. This, however, will soon put them into a state of post-exertional malaise once this has worn off, which can then

contribute to a worsening of the illness, leaving sufferers feel far more unwell than before. Sadly M.E sufferers can over-exert just to live or get through the day. It is therefore important to recognise when you are running on adrenaline – and deal with it by taking it slower. A short term gain is a long term loss in this case.

63. **Feelings of sadness, guilt and loss** – Sufferers may experience these feelings, especially after being diagnosed or becoming ill. With such a change in lifestyle and so many sacrifices that have to be made, it is completely natural to have these feelings. You may grieve for your old life, and feel sad that you cannot do the things that others can do, or what you used to be able to do. Recognise that this is a normal process which happens in many traumatic events such as bereavement.

64. **Cognitive Behavioural Therapy** – This can be offered by a qualified psychologist. Often we find coping with the effects of such an illness can be too much to handle, and understandably you may feel as if you simply cannot cope. Cognitive Behavioural Therapy can help you understand why you feel the way you do, and help you learn techniques in dealing with with the emotional aspects of having the illness. Many sufferers have benefited from it, so if you feel you would, ask your GP to make a referral.

65. **Feeling alone** – M.E can be very isolating, especially when you may have lost your social life and are not able to work. Visits from friends and family can prove exhausting and so you may not see people often. Also difficult is the inability to make solid arrangements due to the fluctuating nature of the illness. Often once we have had the illness for some time, if we rest before any activity and know our limits, we can be fairly sure of what we are able to cope with and so are able to make dates with people. However this is not a fool proof method as you will know, due to the fluctuating nature of the illness, that until you wake up that day you have no idea what symptoms, and the severity of symptoms you will experience. If you are unwell to the extent you cannot see anybody, you may feel very alone, and there are forums for M.E sufferers which offer, as well as information, support in the form of talking to fellow sufferers and sharing information on all aspects of the condition.

Chapter 11: Alternative Therapies

66. **Acupuncture** – A form of ancient Chinese medicine, this method involves inserting fine needles into pressure points of the skin. Although there is no significant evidence that it is helpful in treating M.E, it has been known to improve quality of sleep, and provide some pain relief, both very important factors with the condition.
67. **Aromatherapy** – This is an alternative therapy which uses essential oils to promote wellbeing. The aroma from the oils, when inhaled, is thought to stimulate functioning of the brain, and they can also be absorbed through the skin. As well as being relaxing, there are many different oils available for different ailments. Lavender, for example, promotes sleep – and Neroli is known to help with feelings of depression and anxiety. Burning these before bedtime using an oil burner can often set the mood for sleep by helping to calm the mind.
68. **Chiropractic** – This profession focuses on the bones, muscles and soft tissues of the body and often used spinal stimulation. Sufferers have often found the treatment helpful if there are issues with sore, pulled muscles and joint pain. Where headaches are an issue, this can be due to tension around the neck. Chiropractic treatment aims to make adjustments to the body and so help relieve pain.
69. **Shiatsu** – A Japanese method used to relieve symptoms of poor health which dates back over 4000 years. Commonly used to help relieve symptoms of back pain, it focuses on deep massage. Hand held shiatsu massagers can be purchased online, and they can be used to help relieve muscle tension when you feel your muscles are flaring up.
70. **Homeopathy** – This is a form of alternative medicine which takes a holistic approach (Mind, body and spirit) so looks at the patient as a whole rather than focusing on one area. It takes the approach that 'like treats like', and uses substances usually in tablet form to treat symptoms.
71. **Light Therapy** – This method uses exposure to daylight or specific wavelengths of light. Often used to treat SAD (Seasonal Affective Disorder) it has also been used in cases of M.E. There have been no scientific studies on it, but some sufferers have found it helpful in helping to increase energy levels.
72. **Hypnotherapy** – This is where the mind/body connection comes in. Whereas M.E is primarily a physical illness, the symptoms can be worsened by mental upset. Hypnotherapy can prove helpful in helping to recognize triggers of stress, and deep set

beliefs that have a negative impact on your state of mind. It can help to improve confidence, motivation and self-worth.
73. **Neuro-linguistic Programming** – A method which focuses on the unconscious mind, and the belief that the mind can be 'trained' for the better, hence the word 'programming'. This is particularly important when we look at the 'Fight or flight' response in M.E. As detailed earlier on in the book, it is thought that sufferers are in a near permanent state of the stress response, thus the body produces stress hormones which drain the adrenal gland and lead onto other physical symptoms. The idea of NLP is that the brain is trained to get out of the stress response, giving the body a chance to recover and relieving strain on the immune system.
74. **Pilates** – Developed in the 20th Century, it offers many health benefits. It focuses on core muscles and breathing exercises to relax the mind and body. For someone with M.E who can manage some gentle physical exertion, it can be beneficial in helping to tone and strengthen the muscles. However if stiffness is an issue then this must be approached carefully, and bear in mind that although it is a gentle exercise it can be quite physically demanding for someone with M.E, depending on what your physical abilities are.
75. **Osteopathy** – A profession which focuses on the musculoskeletal system of the body. It not only uses hands on techniques to help treat the symptoms, but looks for the cause of the symptoms also. It can be extremely beneficial for back and neck pain.
76. **Reflexology** – This is an ancient Chinese medicine which focuses on specific parts of the body, which are believed to be linked to major organs. It uses hands on pressure to stimulate these points and thus improve functioning.
77. **Relaxation** – As mentioned previously, relaxation is ideal for M.E sufferers as it not only relaxes the body but the mind too. When mental exertion can be as tiring as physical exertion, relaxation is much recommended so the body as a whole can spend a period expending the least amount of energy possible. Some sufferers find a relaxation session when they feel a crash coming on is helpful. It is a good habit to get into having at least one short session daily, especially when you feel you have over-exerted.

Chapter 12: Symptomatic Relief

78. **Fatigue** – The overwhelming fatigue which is a hallmark of the illness can sometimes be too much to handle. Most sufferers find they get used to it over time, and lots find that they can't remember what it feels like not to be fatigued. When you live with such a burden over time, you become accustomed to it, but this does not mean you should have to let it become you. Although there is little support in terms of healthcare from fatigue there are certain supplements which can help to relieve it. Ones to try are Vitamin B Complex, Co-Enzyme Q-10 and Ginseng, all well known for energy boosting properties. Of course this is not a cure, but even light relief from the dreaded exhaustion can mean the world to someone who suffers from it on a daily basis.
79. **Headaches** – Often M.E sufferers will find that conventional painkillers do little to relieve the Tension headaches common in the illness. Tried and tested among sufferers are different approaches, including head massagers (Or more commonly called, Angels fingers) Headache remedies in stick form which are applied to the temples, or a head and neck massage to help relieve the tension. Co-codamol seems to be the most effective medication-wise for these type of headaches.
80. **Muscle Pain** – The dreaded muscle pain and soreness can wear you down. The most suited painkillers for these are Anti-inflammatories such as Ibuprofen or Diclofenac. For those who painkillers do not work for or prefer a more natural remedy, deep heat rub or muscle bath soak can often provide some relief. Especially effective is Magnesium Oil spray, which when applied directly to the skin can help relax the muscle itself. A T.E.N.S Machine can help provide relief to the pain using Electrical Nerve Stimulation, an alternative form of pain relief, and these can be bought relatively cheaply.
81. **Post-exertional Malaise** – No matter how much we pay for over exertion in terms of crashing, we often pay the consequences again and again. And when the crash hits us, we know about it. The best thing to do as soon as you feel you are crashing is to stop what you are doing, and lay down in a darkened and quietened room. Sometimes sleep is not necessary, the fact your body is resting will help. Epsom salts can be effective at helping reduce the severity of an M.E crash, so a couple of handfuls in the bath will certainly help. A sleep mask can be useful when light sensitivity is an issue.
82. **Hot sweats** – A common symptom of the illness, these can come and go but can be extremely annoying, especially when one is trying to sleep. A hand held fan or a clip on fan can be kept by the bed for these moments! Also helpful is a cool flannel kept nearby.

83. **Sore throats** – A symptoms most if not all sufferers from M.E will be familiar with. Sometimes just talking can make your throat sore! Some sufferers find this symptom appears upon over-exertion, so if you do find your throat is hurting a lot then this may well be the case. A cold drink with ice and throat lozenges can provide relief until it starts to subside, and of course keeping talking to a minimum – easier for some more than others!
84. **Nausea & Vomiting** – There are many different reasons why one with M.E may find the illness is accompanied with nausea and/or vomiting. Where digestive disorders are apparent then this may well be the root cause of the problem, or if vertigo and travel sickness are a significant issue then this could be down to the bodies balance mechanism. Dizziness will often be accompanied by nausea. It is worth visiting your GP if this is a significant issue as medication can be prescribed according to what is causing the problem.
85. **Noise Sensitivity** – A symptom of M.E that sufferers often find overwhelming and distressing. More likely to happen after a crash, it can turn the smallest sound into something which makes your ears physically make popping and thudding noises. Ear plugs of course are recommended at night, but if you are having a day where you are particularly sensitive to noise then wearing these during the day can certainly help. Most friends or relatives are aware that it can be an issue, but often they don't realise how sensitive our ears are, so it can help a lot in blocking the noise out to a level that you can cope with.
86. **Emotional symptoms** – If you feel you indeed have the depression or anxiety that can accompany M.E, then it is recommended to visit your GP If you haven't already. The physical aspects of the illness are distressing enough without dealing with depressive thoughts and feelings on top, so it is important these are dealt with. Ensure you have friends or family you can talk to and get support from when you are feeling down. Often talking about thoughts and feelings can make one feel much better, as problems bottled up are only going to build up.

Chapter 13: Hobbies

87. **Finding hobbies** – Most sufferers after becoming ill can find themselves feeling very isolated due to the limitations of the illness. You may have met up with friends several times a week previously, but now can only manage once every few weeks and for some not at all. Lifestyle changes due to the condition are difficult but there is still a lot you can do inside the home to help take your mind off feeling ill.
88. **Competitions** – Many websites online and magazines offer regular competitions. If you are able to read and access the internet, they can be a great way of passing the time and keeping you occupied. Even better, it's rewarding when you find a winning letter through the post! Be careful though, it can be addictive!
89. **Arts & Crafts** – Art can be very therapeutic and being creative has helped many through different issues. An activity which can be done sat down, it can prove to be relaxing and liberating.
90. **Reading** – If you are reading this book now then you will well know how relaxing reading can be. On the other hand it is informative and with any subject you could ever dream of available there is a huge choice to keep you going. An early night and a good book can really help set you up for a half decent night's sleep.
91. **Meeting friends** – On the occasions you feel well enough to meet with friends it can be so exciting and enjoyable. However it is also likely to prove exhausting. Make things easier by asking friends if they could visit you, and if you cannot tolerate much face to face interaction then keep the meeting short and sweet. It's better to see friends or family briefly than not at all.
92. **Music** – Listening to music can trigger a variety of emotions, thoughts and memories. There are thousands of albums which are designed to be relaxing and therapeutic. Explore these and find something which you like. When stuck inside for a majority of the time, listening to a good album can be a really enjoyable past time.

Chapter 14: Summary

This book will hopefully have provided some valuable information whether you are a sufferer newly diagnosed or a friend/relative who would like to find out more about the condition. It has been written by a fellow sufferer with the intent of helping those who may be feeling isolated and scared after a diagnosis of Myalgic Encephalomyelitis. Of course all every sufferer wants is to get well, and this summary focuses on nothing but that.

93. **Pace, pace and pace again** – The importance of pacing cannot be stressed enough to an M.E sufferer. If you are feeling an *increase* in symptoms then you are not pacing enough. You may find your baseline is extremely low, but this is fine. The idea is that you stay within your limits until you are not feeling an increase in symptoms – and this is the time when you can push a little further to try and increase activity levels gradually.

94. **Get Adequate Rest** – Recognise that watching television or reading is not 'rest' in the eyes of the illness. For most sufferers this is an activity, and of course, activities deplete energy. Devote time each day to get adequate rest in the form of relaxation or simply laying down and having some time in silence by yourself. Even if you are not feeling too bad that day, still try and do this. An afternoon nap can often be the key to getting through the rest of the day.

95. **Focus on your diet** – We all know that diet and nutrition is important for our health, but when you have a chronic illness that importance is magnified. Try and avoid processed food as much as possible, and greasy or sugary foods too. In order for your body to recover you need to have as much nutrition as you possibly can. Of course we all like a treat now and again, but sticking to fresh fruit, vegetables and meat for your main diet is certainly going to help give your body the right fuel it needs.

96. **Learn to say NO** – It is quite well documented that a significant proportion of sufferers appear to have 'Type A' personalities. This makes us driven, ambitious, and more than likely due to this, susceptible to the illness. If you are one of those people who will try and do everything at once and more, then you are likely to fall into this category. You may well have taken the world's problems on your shoulders before you

became ill, but now you need to focus on your health and recognise that any external stressors are likely to have an impact on this. If a task is not life dependent then leave it until tomorrow or when you feel better. It will wait.
97. **Ensure you have a good GP** – When I say 'good' I mean a GP who is familiar with the condition. More often than not the illness is often dismissed as 'Chronic Fatigue' by GP's who have little understanding of it, and some are not supportive. It seems those who do not understand it, find it easier to dismiss it. That is not saying there are not GP's who do understand it, because there are – and those who do are wonderful. A sign a GP is worth having is one who not only looks at symptomatic relief, but who takes an approach to try and help you get better with their input.
98. **Getting the support you need** – You may already be on sickness related benefits due to your condition, or you may be in work – full or part time depending on the severity of your illness. If you feel you are too unwell for work then there is nothing wrong with admitting you need financial help. After all if you try and 'push through' when you have M.E, you will only end up worse off in the long run. If you apply for any welfare then ensure you have professional advice in the form of either the Citizens Advice Bureau or an M.E Support group or organization who provides welfare advice to sufferers. If you have to attend any medical assessments ensure you have someone with you for moral support, and taking note of what is discussed incase this is needed when you get the results.
99. **Having a good support network** – It is helpful to know you have people behind you when you have been diagnosed with the condition. If your family and friends do not know what it is there are lots of leaflets and websites that are designed for the families of M.E sufferers to help educate them and help them to understand what the condition entails. You may find it helpful if they come to medical appointments with you, not only for moral support but to help them to understand. A good friend who takes the time to research and understand the condition from a non-sufferers point of view to help you the best they can, is worth their weight in gold.
100. **Realise you can get better** – Often we hear not so good things about M.E. However it is only usually the relapses we hear about, not the ones who recover. It is completely possible that with the right help and lifestyle changes, you can recover – and many have. Do not listen to people who try and tell you otherwise.
101. **Never give up** – M.E is a very debilitating illness that can literally rip your life apart. It can sometimes feel like it is winning, but you must have faith that no matter how weak

you feel you are always strong enough to fight back as long as you have the right mentality. There are many others fighting it along with you, and so you are not alone. In times of need you may feel desperate and not be able to see ahead, however there is always hope and that's what you need to hold on to. Nothing is impossible!

Poem by the Author

Once I was a fun-loving girl, busy young and free

But my life had to change when I was diagnosed with M.E

It started with a virus, sore throat and fever

I couldn't go to work, or get out of bed either!

Exhausted all the time, something wasn't right

Then I got a diagnosis, and knew I had to fight

I had to give up work, and get a lot of rest

But even when bedbound – I hadn't lost my zest!

When I overdo it, my heart begins to race

I know it can be dangerous, so now I regularly pace

Over-doing it affects me in many different ways

Sometimes I need a nap, others in bed for days

I can't do all of the things that I could do before

I have to make a choice, between every task and chore

It's hard when people see me, and think I look okay,

When my body aches all over and I'm unwell every day

Some days, I feel better, and can do a little more

But if this is too much then I feel worse than before!

I don't know if I will get better, when where or how

But the thing that gets me through the day is positivity somehow

There are many others like me, too many that's for sure

And we all have hope and faith, for the day they find a cure!

Useful Contacts

Action for M.E

P.O Box 2778

Bristol

BS1 9DJ

0845 123 2380

www.actionforme.org.uk

Association of Young People With M.E

AYME

08451 232389

helpline@ayme.org.uk

ME Association

www.meassociation.org.uk

0844 576 5326

Benefits & Work

Benefits & Work Publishing Ltd

PO Box 4352

Warminster

BA12 2AF

office@benefitsandwork.co.uk

www.benefitsandwork.co.uk

ME Research UK

www.meresearch.org.uk

Facebook: ME Research UK

Chronic Fatigue Syndrome Forum

http://www.chronicfatiguesyndrome.me.uk/

References

www.nhs.uk

www.patient.co.uk

www.nice.org.uk

www.ahummingbirdsguide.com

www.drmyhill.co.uk

Printed in Great Britain
by Amazon